Dedicated to Jen Wu, who inspired
many of these revelations.

D1524204

TABLE OF CONTENTS

1. What This Book is About
2. What Are We Seeking, Anyway?
3. How the Universe Works (As Explained by Lego Bricks)
4. Who Are We?
5. How to Lose Weight — Without Getting off the Couch
6. The Healing Power of Rapid Eye Movement
7. Resistance is Futile
8. The Shortcoming of Meditation
9. What "Seinfeld" Says About the Meaning of Life
10. The Toxicity of Distraction
11. How to Deal with the Heaviest Emotion
12. Death, My Best Friend
13. The Paradox of Outcomes and Why Life Isn't Baseball
14. The Demon With 1,000 Faces
15. A Good Exercise to End On

WHAT THIS BOOK
IS ABOUT

How do you start a book like this? Say hello? Wish the reader well? Begin with some gripping tale that grabs the reader by the throat?

Well, I'll say hello, and I do wish you well. As for the last part, maybe I'll just tell you what this book is and why I wrote it.

As far as what this book is, which is simple enough – this book is a series of essays. Each one covers an idea that changed how I think, how I understand the world and, ultimately, how I live my life.

The essays don't form a singular narrative, and each (mostly) stands on its own, although I'd recommend reading them in the order presented. The reason being, first, occasionally essays refer back to a previous essay. Second, more importantly, I believe they are in an order that makes them the easiest to process.

The essays themselves aren't particularly long and are written conversationally. I wrote them that way because I believe that makes the ideas within them as accessible as possible.

I'll let you decide if that's true.

As far as why I wrote this book – for the first 35 years of my life, I lived in darkness. This darkness caused me anxiety, rage, guilt, fear; even feelings of not wanting to exist.

I felt this way subtly all the time, with the feelings getting louder at night. I didn't sleep well. My mind tended to race. And I never felt fully happy with myself.

I was, as Thoreau said, living a life of silent desperation.

In March 2020, at the onset of the coronavirus pandemic, I hit rock-bottom. I crashed. And I realized I couldn't live life this way anymore.

In the months that followed, thanks to the right teachers at the right time, I realized truths about this world that I never realized before. And I unlearned literally hundreds of false beliefs, which were keeping me in a prison of my own creation.

Today, I am a happier, healthier, more successful person. My fears, my anger, my anxiety and my guilt have vastly diminished. And my gratitude, my happiness and my understanding of the world have all increased.

I wrote this book because I don't think I'm the only one to ever be stuck in darkness. I think many of us struggle with so many things in our lives unnecessarily, simply because we don't know what's real.

I wrote this book to show what's real. My hope is, based on that, you'll be able to shed what's not. That matters because, in my experience, attachment to what's not real is the cause of our suffering.

I assure you, the goal of this book is not to tell you what to do or how to think. In fact, it's the exact opposite – the goal of this book is to empower you to be yourself and to only do what you know is right.

My aspiration – this book advances your own spiritual journey toward your own awakening. It gives you a deeper understanding of the world, your true motivations and your true self.

Have fun. I hope you enjoy the book.

WHAT ARE WE SEEKING, ANYWAY?

There's a great scene in the show *Mad Men* where the main character, Don Draper, tells a prospective client he's pitching, "You're on top and you don't have enough. You're happy, because you're successful – for now. But what is happiness? It's a moment before you need more happiness."

I love this monologue because it encapsulates exactly how I lived my life for a long time. Constantly seeking. Occasionally getting, which led to momentary satisfaction.

And then, seeking again.

My career is a good example. I was always seeking something – a better job, more money, a loftier title; or short-term goals like getting a project done well. I'd often feel as if I couldn't rest or even enjoy myself until I accomplished whatever I was focused on at the time.

I was a hard worker, so I often got what I was seeking. But did that bring me satisfaction?

For a brief period. Then, I'd find something new to pursue, and not feel good about myself until I got it.

A perfect illustration – between 2013 and 2017, thanks to getting better jobs, I managed to triple my salary. And yet, despite that success, I didn't feel any happier. Instead, my mind was always focused on getting recognition for whatever project I was working on in that moment and moving up.

The point is, no matter what happened, I was always after the next thing. Always seeking.

This pattern existed within my relationships as well. When I wasn't in a relationship, I'd seek one, because that's what a person is supposed to do: be in a relationship. Then, when I'd get into a relationship, I'd seek validation from my partner. Even with my friends, seeking validation via their laughter.

When I spoke, I spoke with seeking in mind. To prove I'm smart. To prove I'm funny. To prove that the other side is wrong.

It was just like Don Draper said. Happiness for me was nothing more than an ephemeral sensation that was quickly followed by the need for more happiness.

What's the psychology behind this?

I'm sure you've already figured it out. I was seeking something because I felt like I wasn't good enough as I was. Only by acquiring something from someone else – a laugh, a promotion, praise – would I feel worthy.

Of course, that worthiness was temporary and, when it left, those feelings of being less-than would come back. And the seeking cycle would repeat.

Despite it being so obvious now, for most of my time on earth I never stopped to reflect on what I was doing. I figured, of course you should have goals. This seeking was good, because it provided motivation. And you don't just sit around, you take on the impossible.

I know now there is no happiness with this logic. In fact, it wasn't even a good path for me to maximize my potential.

Instead, all it led to was suffering, as it caused me to always feel bad about myself.

How did I finally end this cycle? It happened on the day I suffered most.

Mid-March 2020, San Francisco. COVID-19 had just caused everyone to take refuge in their homes. Nobody knew how bad the virus was, what it meant or how it would end. Our world was filled with speculation and alarm.

Me, I switched to working from home, with my job becoming busier than ever. And my 18-month relationship with my live-in girlfriend, Jen, was at its lowest point. There was fighting and constant tension caused by my own anger, my own insecurity, my persistent seeking; i.e., my own inability to feel good about myself.

That was bad enough. It was taken to another level thanks to botched LASIK eye surgery, with my right eye turning the color of a stop sign. It felt like a dagger had been jammed in there and someone was swirling around the blade.

That proved to be the ultimate dilemma for someone with my mental pattern – all I was seeking at that point was to rub my eye. But of course, the doctor said the one thing I absolutely couldn't do was rub my eye.

I was not handling it well.

It got so bad that Jen drove me to see an ophthalmologist. On the car ride there, instead of being gracious to her for her help, somehow, all of this became her fault. I exploded at her.

Except this time, for the first time in our relationship, soft-spoken Jen exploded back. She told me it was over. She told me I could take my bad attitude, my dour outlook and temper, and split.

We never even made it to the doctor. Instead, I went back home, turned off the lights in my bedroom, and lay in my bed. As I lay there, it sank in – I had self-destructed. Again.

There were two options. The first was not to change anything internally and everything externally; start anew and escape. That option would've led to another self-destruction a few years down the road.

The second option was to look inside. To make real, internal change. Somewhat reluctantly, with very little confidence I could pull it off, I told Jen I was willing to put the work in.

I honestly thought it wouldn't matter. That she was going to leave me anyway. And that it wouldn't work.

But Jen, thankfully, didn't leave me. Instead, she helped me get rid of so much. That's a good thing, because there's no way I could've done it by myself.

Over the next three months, quarantined in our San Francisco home during a national lockdown, Jen helped me understand why I was so desperately seeking so many different things. And she taught me how to let things go.

It was a time of great unlearning.

Most of the time, I wasn't even aware I was seeking anything. I was just bothered by something. But, almost invariably, when Jen and I talked through why I was bothered by that thing, it was because I was seeking something and fearful about not getting it.

I'll use work as an example again. I would feel a tremendous amount of stress at work if I got in a disagreement with a colleague. Outwardly, I was cool, but internally it would run in my mind over and over.

That inner conflict prevented me from being in the present and shortened my patience.

To get through it, Jen would ask me why I was feeling that way.

I'd give a reason, and she'd ask why again. Over and over, until we found the root cause.

With a work conflict, after scraping away the superficial, I'd admit the conflict bothered me because I wanted to prove I'm right (subtext – because I am right). Then Jen would ask, why do you need to be proven right?

Because … And then I'd have to do some soul-searching. The honest answer was that because if I'm wrong, it meant that I'd be shown to others to be wrong. And that would reaffirm to them what I already knew – I don't really deserve this job, I am not good enough and now people will know I'm not good enough.

What Jen did next was interesting. Most people here will say, "Paul, you are good enough. You accomplished this, this and this. You are a smart, good person."

That's a well-meaning thing to say, but it would've solved nothing. It's a band-aid that would've made me feel good in the moment, but the problem would've persisted.

Instead, Jen confronted me with the worst-case scenario. She'd ask me, in this case, what it would mean if people knew I wasn't good enough. If they saw me as less-than, saw me as I was seeing myself.

That's when things got interesting. I began to think – what does it even mean to be good enough? What standard was I holding myself to? And who was enforcing that standard?

Those questions helped me realize the real conflict was with myself. I was telling myself that I needed to live a certain way and do certain things to be worthy – to myself.

That made me realize that to fix this conflict, I didn't need anything to change externally. All I needed was to drop this belief that I needed to be a certain way to be happy with myself. And instead, just allow myself to be.

Painstakingly, while the conclusion was usually the same, I had to go through this across a variety of issues. I will say that sometimes, I needed to do something externally to fix a situation, although usually that was incredibly obvious once I boiled away all the other stuff.

Most of the time though, I just needed to let go of some arbitrary standard I was giving myself, based on a fear that wasn't real. After I let it go, that particular conflict would go away, my mind would become clearer and I'd feel happier.

Jen was patient with me. We went through issue after issue, clearing these hollow desires from my body. The process continues to this day.

Here's the bigger point. Back to the Don Draper quote in the beginning.

In my old world, Don Draper was right. Happiness was something I sought, something I fought for.

After I began seeing holes in that thinking, I started asking myself – what's actually stopping me from being happy right now?

It was never anything external. It was never that I didn't have an impressive title or because of something someone said or because I needed a higher salary. No, the only thing that was preventing me from being happy in any given moment was – well – me.

Crazy, when you think about it. How we make our lives so unnecessarily complicated.

That said, I couldn't just say "I'm happy now" and magically be happy. I had to go through the hard work of really understanding why I was suffering, identifying the fear that's causing the suffering and then letting that fear go.

Here's what I realized from all of this – I would push myself to the ends of the earth and work my fingers to the bone trying to achieve Don Draper's definition of happiness. And still, I'd never be happy, because this approach assumes I needed to get happiness from somewhere else.

This is wrong, a false belief. Because happiness doesn't come externally, and it isn't something I could earn after I did something. Instead, I realized happiness is my natural state. To live in my natural state consistently, I just needed to let go of all the attachments that were bringing me out of it and causing me unhappiness.

Bottom line, all I needed to be happy was to allow myself to be. No accomplishments needed.

HOW THE UNIVERSE WORKS (AS EXPLAINED BY LEGO BRICKS)

Roughly 13.8 billion years ago, according to the experts, the Big Bang happened.

What was that like?

Basically, some force threw a big box of Lego bricks across the floor. And they rolled out every which way – in fact, according to the latest research on the universe expanding, they are still rolling away.

But the Lego bricks in the box opposed this. They hate being separated from the other bricks. Despite them being so violently thrown apart, they are focused on getting back together.

This desire toward togetherness manifests via gravity, one of the most powerful forces in the universe. Gravity is still mysterious; Einstein hypothesized that it's the weight of heavy objects bending the fabric of time and space. When I think about it, it seems like magic – objects having an effect on other objects millions of miles away.

Not so much different than the force in "Star Wars."

Either way, gravity works to undo the work of the Big Bang. Lego bricks are violently thrown across the floor. Over time, because of gravity, they come back together and form larger and larger structures. But then something will come along and kick over that structure, scattering the pieces across the floor.

And the process repeats. I see this trend over and over.

Take life on earth. What we call life on Earth is nothing more than a collection of complex Lego structures. The Lego bricks on this planet joined together over millions of years and formed things like kangaroos, giraffes and humans.

But we've had many minor Big Bangs here on Earth that have violently destroyed all of those structures. The best example is the meteor that killed all the dinosaurs – in one instant, all those beautiful, complex Lego structures across our planet were destroyed, their parts scattered across our world.

Good news for us – the bricks eventually reformed into us. If it weren't for that meteor, we would've never been created.

We ourselves might be the first Earth species to create our own Big Bang. A world war, particularly one that used nuclear weapons, would probably do the trick. Imagine that – the Lego structures become so complex, they actually decide to destroy themselves.

We see this pattern emerge within our physical desires as well. Over many weeks or many years, we slowly gain influence over the Lego bricks around us. And then, occasionally – often caused by an out-of-control desire to dominate over Lego bricks – a big violent event will come by and destroy that connection.

Money is a good illustration. By working hard, we slowly amass more and more money, which we use to buy more and more Lego structures. Except sometimes we can lose big amounts of this money in one singular event – a stock market crash, a scam, a stupid gamble.

Relationships tend to follow the same pattern, even more so. Over time, we slowly build trust with the Lego structures around us.

But occasionally, an event – cheating, lying, stealing – can destroy the relationship, and those two complex Lego structures go spiraling into other directions.

Here's the point – in the physical world, we are driven by the physical desire to gain influence over other Lego bricks. Of undoing the Big Bang, of it all being back together, with us on top.

Except what would happen if we ever accomplished our goal? If we ever actually did get everything back together again, and put all the Lego bricks in the box, with us on top?

Well, all of that pressure would cause us and everything else in this universe to explode into another Big Bang. Another scattering of these Lego bricks all over the room, only for them to want to come back together again.

And that's exactly what happens. Everything is scattered apart, everything comes together, over and over, on various scales.

When you step back and see the physical world for what it is, it seems pretty pointless. Correction – it is entirely pointless. No matter what we do, no matter how much money we make, no matter how people feel about us, no matter how many followers we get or how many people we "influence," everything will be destroyed and rebuilt and destroyed 10,000 times over and none of it will ever matter.

Inspirational, right? Yet it's the truth of the physical world.

The good news – there is more to the universe than just the Lego bricks, aka the physical world. There also exists another, more interesting world we call consciousness.

We have lots of ideas about consciousness. Some say this is created by God, others by Allah, others by Judah; and people fight wars about that. I think it's fair to say we don't know exactly who created it, at least not yet, or what it really is.

But even the most reluctant scientist will admit that consciousness does exist. Descartes said it best – I think, therefore I am. In fact, consciousness is the only thing in this world we know for sure exists.

The real question is this – is our minds, and this feeling of consciousness, just an unintended and quite unnecessary byproduct of the proverbial Lego bricks coming together in a usual way that gives us the power of thought?

Maybe. Most scientists would say so. That what we think, what we feel, and all of our deepest emotions and most profound experiences are nothing more than an evolutionary accident. That the only real reason we have the brains we have is to give us an advantage in the jungle.

I consider myself a rational man. That's a very rational explanation. Not a particularly inspiring one, but a rational one.

Although, there's a big part of me that doesn't believe it.

The science crowd will say that part of me is driven by fear. That we refuse to accept that our lives are nothing more than the unusual arrangement of these comic Lego bricks. That the truth is we don't matter, nothing matters, and we'll all be forgotten soon enough.

Except there have been experiences in my life that have transcended rational explanation.

One example – for years, I struggled with what I should do with my life. Then, one night, I woke up and had this overwhelming urge to write. It was a calling; a message I received that felt like nothing I'd experienced before or since.

From that point forward, I've focused on being a writer, which has led to great success. Why did that idea come to me – was it my rational mind finally figuring out my biggest struggle or some deeper force showing me the way?

The science crowd would say the former; in my heart I know it's the latter.

Additionally, I've had many times in my life where I cannot solve a problem or I'm not sure what to do. It's only when I stop thinking about it, when I let go of the problem and allow the universe to answer, do I get clarity.

Scientists have probably done some research to explain how this works. Maybe it makes sense. But, in my heart, I know there's something bigger at work.

A better example: I had a conversation with my mom once about the death of her mother, my grandmother. Shortly after her mom died, my mother said she saw a white butterfly in her garden. She had never seen a white butterfly before nor since in her garden.

She obviously had experienced great sadness over the death of her mother. But when she saw that white butterfly, she knew that was her mother trying to talk to her in some way that simply could not be explained.

It gave her peace. She knew, in that moment, her mother was in a better place.

And then there are the countless accounts of people who have been declared clinically dead for a short period of time and were resuscitated. These near-death experiences have been formally studied and people's descriptions of death are eerily similar: The feeling of their soul leaving their body. Moving toward a white light. All of their worries and concerns were erased. A lightness of being; a feeling of euphoria. Some even report speaking directly to a higher power.

The science crowd has countered these experiences by saying they are merely delusions. To me, there are too many similarities in all of these stories to just brush them off.

But forget all of those examples from other people. Let me ask you a question: Have you ever had an experience that simply cannot be explained by science? Perhaps an intuition. A message received from a loved one who was either far away or passed on. A calling of some sort, or a coincidence or string of luck that led to a life-changing event?

Think about that moment, if you had one. Do you believe that came from this physical world? Or from another place entirely, beyond explanation?

I'm thinking many of you had. It's a shared human experience, this feeling of something almost otherworldly. I'd argue that's exactly what it is – it is our connection to the spiritual realm.

Quick qualification – I have nothing but respect for scientists. They've done an amazing job understanding the physical world and all the technologies that make this world better are only possible because of them. I think we should listen to them when it comes to physical matters; they are amazing pioneers in furthering human knowledge.

But I don't believe there has been the same study into the spiritual world. In fact, I think it's been mocked by many, despite most of us having experiences that defy reasonable explanation. I believe there's shame involved here, as people are questioning other people because they themselves are questioning their own experience.

Either way, let's assume, for the sake of argument, that there is indeed a spiritual realm we call consciousness. And this consciousness is beyond the physical world that our bodies and brains inhabit.

Now, go back to what I wrote about the physical world. Everything in this universe is made from the same stuff. Humans, rocks, billy goats, stars, moons, ice cream – all are created from the same matter that created this universe. The stuff is just rearranged in different ways.

If this spiritual world exists, you tell me what's more likely – humans are rearranged in such a perfect way that only we can tap into this spiritual world. Or, that all things can experience this spiritual world, and what we as humans experience every day is the human version of that, processed by the tools we have – i.e., our brains and bodies.

To me, logic suggests the latter. To me, it's far more likely that all matter in this universe experiences consciousness, as opposed to us humans hitting the Lego jackpot and being the only creatures able to do so.

And then I go a step further. Is this consciousness unique to us? In other words, do we all have our own conscious, our own spirit?

Or, is there just one consciousness, one spiritual realm, that we all tap into? How we process that experience depends on the tools our physical body has – primarily, for us humans, what's in our brains – but there's just one consciousness. There's just one spiritual realm we all share.

To me, once again, it's far more likely we all share one consciousness. We all tap into it, and while our experience differs dramatically depending on how we interpret it, it's all the same.

Picture this – all of these Lego bricks spread across a carpeted floor. All of those Lego bricks have their own unique relationship with the carpet on the floor, all thinking that their particular piece of carpet is unique to them.

Except it isn't. The carpet is shared by all the Lego bricks. It's the realm beyond the physical world that keeps it all together.

That, to me, is what's really going on. All of us are a collection of Lego bricks in a physical world. The physical world is ever-changing, with these physical forces constantly either bringing things toward us or pushing them away from us.

Contract, expand. Contract, expand. That's what the physical world does.

It all sits on this spiritual world, which is the carpet. And the carpet doesn't move. It's ever-present, always still, possessing complete knowledge.

When we die, the Lego bricks merely break apart and form into something else, which once again has its own unique experience with the carpet. We then become attached to that experience and fear losing it when we die.

Except we don't lose it, do we? Because it isn't ours to gain or lose. It merely is. And it isn't just for us, it's for all the Lego structures in the room, regardless of how they are formed.

All of this raises questions. Like, why does the carpet even bother with the Lego? I don't know, maybe the carpet was bored. Or, who created this whole thing to begin with? I don't know that one either.

Here's what I do know though – the carpet is the important thing, not the Lego. Don't get tied down on the needs and wants of the Lego, as all of those are temporary. And most of those urges will ultimately lead to destruction.

Instead, tap into the carpet, which is best done by quieting your mind and really listening. That's where the true purpose is.

Listen to that, and you'll find your true purpose, your true meaning. And it'll be far more compelling than endless expansion and destruction.

WHO ARE WE?

In the United States, the most accepted story of our existence is the Christian story. Let's analyze it for a minute to answer the question at the top of this essay.

We all know the Christian story – after we die, our soul is judged and then we are sent to heaven or hell for eternity. Hence, be good.

Let's focus on the soul part for a minute. According to the Christian story, our physical body obviously dies when we die. But the soul lives on, which is the real us, and has a direct relationship with God.

Another question – where does heaven and hell exist? Just south of Del Boca Vista?

No, of course not. Our bodies exist in the physical world and cannot go to heaven or hell. Only our souls can go to heaven or hell in the spiritual world.

Okay, assuming all of that is fact, back to the question at the top of this essay. According to the Christian story, who are we?

Well, we aren't our physical bodies. Because even after our physical bodies die, we live on.

Instead, Christians would say the real "us" is our souls, which are not even confined to this world. They merely inhabit this world for a short period of time.

After that time ends, according to Christian belief, we go somewhere else in the spiritual world.

Continuing on, Christian belief says the physical body is little more than a clump of matter that has sinful urges like gluttony, greed and lust. Christians instead work to transcend the needs of the body and listen to the real us, the spirit.

This is, according to Christian belief, our fundamental internal struggle. This conflict between the false physical body and our real spiritual self.

Let me abruptly shift topics. Whenever I hear a successful person interviewed, they seem to always give the same advice: some version of "follow your heart." I've never heard a successful person say, "follow your brain."

Objectively, "follow your heart" is a dumb statement. Your heart is basically just a muscle tasked with pumping blood throughout your body. It isn't capable of thinking or communicating to you in any way.

No, "heart" here is clearly a metaphor for something we cannot accurately define. It's just a figure of speech we use because we aren't sure where these directions come from and we are certain it doesn't come from our brains.

And yet, if you listen to successful people, they will say listening to this force – whatever it is, wherever it comes from – is the key to happiness. Much the same way Christians say listen to your spirit, not the flesh.

Once again, it's that same dichotomy. Ignore the immediate urges of the body and instead focus on the lasting wisdom of the soul.

What's the point I'm trying to make?

To understand this world and to be successful in it, we must first understand who we are. Otherwise, it's hard to get anywhere if you don't even know where you are.

So, who are we?

Well, according to Christians and most other religions, they will say you aren't actually a human being on planet Earth. You are a spiritual being briefly inhabiting a physical body. After that body dies, you move on.

This follows the advice of so many successful people. They seem to all say the same thing – focus on the soul, not the brain or the body. Tap into who you really are.

Take a minute and think about that – if that's true, it means the real us is an undying force that isn't confined to this world. That's pretty wild.

Better question – what does this mean?

Well, it means a lot of things. Here's one thing – we obviously need to take care of our bodies in the same way we need to take care of our cars. To live a good life, we must eat well, exercise, keep our minds clear; just like if we want to have a reliable automobile, we need to change our oil frequently and occasionally replace the tires and brakes.

Our problems begin when our body overtakes who we really are, and we begin to think our body is our truth. With this power, the body will always chase temporary satisfaction, which leads to suffering.

This makes sense, because our bodies are temporary. Compare that to our souls, which are eternal. Which is why the soul is concerned about lasting outcomes, like love and true wealth and enduring happiness, whereas our bodies just want the quick fix.

Additionally, by understanding who we really are, we are allowed to see things from the proper perspective. And, as a general rule, that means letting things go.

I'll use a personal and timely example to illustrate my point. Right now, I want a promotion at work. I have a good job, but it annoys me that people I think don't work as hard or as well as I do have higher titles than me. At times, it has consumed my thinking.

This is very much a concern of the flesh. The quicker I can let it go, the better.

Here are things the soul would care about in this exact situation: Does the job I do each day make me happy? How can I best serve the world through my role? What are the things I need to get better at to make more of an impact?

Ironically, by focusing on these things, I will actually see much more success at work and ultimately be more successful. And, I'll be happier doing it.

Even take it down to the day-to-day stuff. The body, in a work setting, is constantly worried about its place in the world, how other people see it and proving itself as right.

This leads to a tremendous amount of energy wasted throughout the day and a whole lot of stress. Meanwhile the soul doesn't care about any of that stuff and avoids all of that stress, as the soul is just focused on doing its best.

In relationships, it's similar. The body, which *is not* the real you, is always focused on gaining the upper hand in relationships. It is focused on getting power, winning arguments and quick thrills, but is never actually happy.

The soul, which again *is* the real you, doesn't worry about any of those things. And the soul is always happy.

Clearly, listening to the soul is the path to true happiness. It then becomes a matter of how.

Throughout this book, I'll write about techniques that can rid your consciousness of the attachments of the body. By cleaning out that clutter, what's left is the real you, the soul.

More to come there. The key takeaway from this piece – know who you are. Who you really, truly are – a spiritual force experiencing this world through a human body.

Understanding that is the first step toward inner peace.

HOW TO LOSE WEIGHT — WITHOUT GETTING OFF THE COUCH

When I was 31, fresh off a breakup, I moved to San Francisco.

I was single, I had a good job and I was in a new, exciting city. What a dream! The world was my oyster; a whole new chance to start a new life.

My first two-and-a-half years in SF, I did do a lot of things you'd expect me to do. I dated, I made new friends, I tried new things, I tried new foods, I seriously traveled for the first time, all of that. On paper, it all looked good.

For the most part, it was. Except there was something that prevented me from enjoying it as much as I could've: expectations.

Where I worked, I was the only single one. Even people younger than me were all married. They all were beginning to have kids. When I asked about their weekends, they talked of surviving on little sleep and going to kids' parties.

I talked about the Ben & Jerry's flavor I got at the corner store that Friday.

I was also the only single one in my family. My brother and sisters all had children and significant others. Every holiday was everyone with their tribes, me by myself.

This, as you guessed, caused me to feel embarrassed for being single. Nobody in my family, my friends or my work made me feel that way – it came from myself. And yet I somehow felt like I was letting people down, that I was expected to be in a relationship now and start a family, as if I was less-than for not checking those boxes.

The irony, of course, is there are many married guys with kids who would love the freedom I had. The grass is greener, as they say.

As the tale always goes, only when I dropped this expectation about dating did I find someone I wanted to start a relationship with.

There's nothing new in the story I just told; that's the exact lesson of every Hallmark rom-com.

Instead, I'd love to take a look at where this stress came from in the first place. There's a clear source – expectations; those magical, mythical devils that destroy happiness, take you from the moment and ensure a bad time.

For my money, there's no cheesecake, no nacho bowl, no triple-decker pizza that makes you feel heavier than the weight of expectations. By shedding them, you'll feel Rihanna-fit.

And you don't even have to get off the couch.

What are expectations, anyway?

Sometimes, I think about all us humans are expected to do, and the weight is crumbling.

We're expected to marry by a specific time, have kids by a specific time, start a career – not a job – by a specific time, be grateful, stay calm, say certain things, not say other certain things, keep some interests, keep a well-adorned home, raise kids a specific way, keep up a great social media presence, decorate our homes for Christmas, stay informed …

I could keep going and going. It never ends.

And then there are the expectations we have for ourselves, which can be far heavier than any other. Look a certain way, act a certain way, make other people somehow feel a certain way, etc., etc., etc.

And then, there are the expectations we have for circumstances. Our wedding will be perfect. Our Thanksgiving dinner will be perfect. Our date night with our spouse will be perfect. Our vacation perfect. Our night out with friends perfect, never a dull or awkward moment; constant joy.

And then, far too often, there are our expectations for everyone else. Expecting our parents to be interested in every minute detail of our lives. Expecting our spouse to be supportive and always say the exact right thing. Expecting our boss to always think of us when they act. Our friends, too.

It goes on and on. You might even have expectations right now for how this experience is supposed to go (I apologize in advance for letting you down).

Sometimes, it gets to the point where I think we think we're in some sort of movie. People are breathlessly watching our every move, judging every subtle action we take. If we don't hit the perfect notes, our story isn't exactly perfect and the audience will be disappointed.

We can't let the audience be disappointed! They have expectations, and we must live up to those, no matter what.

The point – I don't think there's more of anything in this world than expectations. They suck up so much of our mental energy, I wonder how there's room for our brains to do anything else.

The most ironic part of all of this? Our expectations are almost never met.

Our date night with our spouse was nice, sure, but it wasn't perfect. Certainly not as perfect as the Instagram post made it appear.

Our "dream job" is good, sure. But the boss is kind of annoying and a lot of the work can be pretty boring.

Even big events, like holidays or weddings, come with such high expectations. We feel a lot of stress beforehand because the expectations are so high. And yet, when they are over, at times, there can be a sense of emptiness, too.

Here's the reality – life is long. Most of our lives are pretty boring. Maybe we're doing work or we're just sitting and watching TV or driving somewhere or doing some chore. Those moments take up far more time than anything else.

That reality clashes with this desire to live a glamourous, exotic, amazing, astonishing life. There's conflict there.

Plus, there's conflict we feel about not meeting society's expectations. My example of being single past 30 is a common one. So is not having kids at the typical time or your career not taking off on schedule.

I want to flip it around. Let's say you hit all the expectations you feel society is putting on you; you check every box. Surely, if you do that, you'll feel an overwhelming sense of euphoria, right?

Umm ... no. Lots of times, after we check those boxes, we get this sensation that our life isn't really even ours.

That causes depression. It can even cause us to have this overwhelming desire to get the hell out of there, change your name, grow out your beard and spend the rest of your life woodworking in the foothills of New Hampshire (or perhaps that's just me).

We set expectations we almost never meet. In the rare times we do meet them, we feel such a severe sense of anguish about others dictating our life, we want to burn down everything and start anew.

Why again do we set these expectations?

That leads to a more interesting question – where do all these expectations come from?

Some, I suppose, come from our parents and our culture. But where did our parents and our culture get them from?

When you analyze it, they all stem from insecurities.

That's also true of the expectations we put on ourselves. They all are a direct result of our perceived shortcomings; the feeling that somehow, if we act perfect or achieve a perfect result, we'll somehow feel better about ourselves.

These expectations all come from a place of pain. And yet, I see such stickiness with them.

They come into our lives without us ever questioning why they are there. But to get rid of them takes an overwhelming amount of logic, personal experience and effort, to the point that most of us just keep them around.

It's like some guy suddenly appears in your kitchen, demanding you make him pancakes, a steak dinner and banana pudding. For some reason, you feel compelled to make this stranger all of these things, only for him to criticize them all for not being good enough. Undeterred, he gives more orders, and – God knows why – you keep acting upon them, but no matter how well you make a specific dish, he still complains.

Soon, feeding this man becomes the biggest focus of your life. He grows fatter and fatter and you grow wearier and wearier.

None of it makes any sense, but you see everyone else feeding this man, too. So you keep doing it, figuring it's the normal thing to do.

Well, it's time to kick this fat man out of your kitchen. You don't even remember giving him permission to enter in the first place. He's doing nothing for you. And, quite frankly, he's rude.

You'll feel so much lighter without him in your life. And then, even the times you do actually want to make banana pudding, you make it for yourself, and it tastes damn good.

In the beginning of this piece, I said that once I stopped hoping for a relationship, I found one. Same is true for everything – once you stop expecting to live a happy life, you'll live one.

THE HEALING POWER OF RAPID EYE MOVEMENT

End of August, 2020. The scene – Montana's Glacier National Park. Which, for my money, is the most beautiful national park in the country. A cross between Switzerland and Alaska.

The crown jewel of the park is the Going-to-the-Sun Road. While it starts as a placid drive around Lake McDonald, it turns spectacular when you hit "The Loop," which is when the road narrows to a sliver and climbs 3,200 feet of elevation.

As you drive up, one side is mountain. The other is sheer cliff; thousands of feet above the valley below.

The road, for many, is breathtakingly beautiful. A stunning look at some of the best mountain scenery North America has to offer.

For me, it was pure terror.

Some context: I hate heights. I'm fine, I'm fine, I'm fine, and then once I hit a certain elevation, it all goes to hell. I freeze up, go into panic mode and think of nothing but getting the hell out of there.

I hate it. It's embarrassing. But I can't get rid of it.

Three days earlier, I went to Glacier alone, and tried to drive the Going-to-the-Sun Road. Halfway through, the heights overwhelmed me. Feeling beyond frustrated, I turned around and went back home, tail between my legs.

This time I resolved to be different. I was with Jen and didn't want to show that kind of weakness in front of my girlfriend. But, as we began the climb up to the loop, the fear hit me – and my faux-manliness faded into quiet, unnerving panic.

Jen sensed it. Told me to pull over. Right there, in the car, we did a quick eye movement exercise.

Right after, I began the drive again. The fear – completely gone. We spent the day hiking around the highest points of the park, seeing all kinds of cliffs that just hours before would've put me into a state of horror.

Now, I felt nothing, other than amazement seeing it all. It was just one example of how rapid eye movement has helped improve my life.

Okay, reading what I just wrote, you are probably wondering: What is "rapid eye movement" and how exactly has it improved my life?

Prepare to be disappointed.

Here's how it works. You think of something that you want to get rid of. In my example, it's my fear of heights. But it doesn't have to be a fear, necessarily – it could be a grudge, anger over something, etc.

The key is it must be specific. The more specific the thought is, the more likely it'll work.

OK, so you have your thought you need to get rid of. Here's where it gets weird.

Have someone else – in the Glacier case, Jen – sit in front of you. And have that person stick out their finger and move it back and forth in front of your face.

Your job – sit there, think of that thought you want to get rid of, and follow the finger without moving your head. Left and right, left and right, your eyes should go. If you are doing it right, you'll literally feel the feeling leave your body.

Oftentimes my eyes water and sometimes my body will jolt while I'm doing this. You can usually follow the finger for a minute or so before you get a little dizzy and need to rest.

Break for about a minute and do it again.

Repeat over and over until the feeling is gone – usually takes around five to six tries. Afterward, I'm usually exhausted. But the feeling has left my body.

At this point, I'm sure you are thinking … errrr, what.

Trust me, that was my reaction when Jen's mom first did it to me. I was highly skeptical, thinking it was some pseudoscience like astrology or healing crystals.

Except this worked. Immediately. Now, I even do it by myself. I'll just lie in bed, think of a feeling I want to get rid of and move my eyes rapidly back-and-forth. If I'm disciplined enough with it, it'll be gone.

Here's just a partial list of the things I was able to clear from my mind using this technique –

- Fear of heights, as described.
- Fear of flying.
- Unspoken grudges I'd held onto for years.
- Work stress from various situations.
- Fear of making the wrong decision.
- Anger… lots of anger.
- Many, many more (I can't remember them all because, well, they're gone).

Despite all of this success, every time I do it, I go in with a cynical mind. Despite that, each time it works, I feel mentally lighter afterwards, and I'm happy I did it.

Obvious reaction to what I just wrote: "You're kidding, right?"

I assure you, I am not.

What I described above is an amateur version of eye movement desensitization and reprocessing (EMDR), a technique that has proved to be successful in treating chronic trauma like PTSD.

I want to be completely clear here – the actual EMDR process is far more rigorous, far more structured and more effective. If you have severe trauma, like PTSD, please go to a professional to get it done.

Instead, what I shared is a version of rapid eye movement I'm doing to treat amateur-level trauma, like being annoyed at an annoying coworker. For me, the process I've described has been more beneficial to me than literally anything else I've ever tried for getting rid of those hard-to-get-rid-of thoughts.

I'm sure you are wondering – why would rapid eye movement work? The short answer is scientists aren't sure, but they're actively researching.

There's a theory that it works because it degrades your working memory of a thought and that removes any strong feelings you have about it. Another, which makes sense to me, is that it replicates what happens during REM sleep, which is when your brain processes information.

Regardless, it appears that rapid eye movement somehow helps you process thoughts in a way that desensitizes you to it. Then, when those thoughts arise again – say, thinking of something that someone did to you at work – you don't have the same strong emotions attached to it.

All I know is what I've experienced. And I can honestly say it's improved my life. I now do it at least twice a week to keep my mind clear.

Part of me feels guilty that I do it. It feels like I'm using a "cheat code" to get rid of big issues.

I will say, for it to work, you need to find the true root cause by continuing to ask yourself why. You need to know why you feel a specific way. The more clarity, the better.

That takes hard work. The problem was I used to do that hard work – get to the root cause, admit things I didn't want to admit – and the thought would still be there. It was frustrating to me that, even though I had uncovered the root cause, I still could not let go of it.

That's where rapid eye movement fits in. For me, it works as a swift sword cut that removes a polyp from my mind. And I can't tell you how refreshing it feels when that thought finally leaves my body and I can walk around feeling far lighter.

Will it work for you?

I believe it will. All I can say is, approach it with an open mind. For me, it's been such a wonderful tool to have – I couldn't have made this journey without it.

RESISTANCE IS FUTILE

Several months ago, I was talking with someone close to me. This person – I'll call him Ron – said he had had a recurring dream since he was a child where he was hiding in a garage from some unseen evil force coming after him.

Ron never actually saw this force coming after him. Instead, whenever Ron felt it coming near, he would wake up in a state of crippling fear.

Ron had this dream at least once a month for as long as he could remember.

To counter, I had Ron close his eyes and put himself back in the dream. Again, he envisioned himself in the garage, again feeling this overwhelming sense of dread from this unknown force coming after him.

Except this time, I told Ron not to open his eyes, no matter what. Instead, I told him to confront the force.

Ron struggled as the evil force entered the garage. As I watched him with his eyes closed, he was clearly overtaken by fear. In his mind, he wanted to look away and find a place to hide; anything but face the dread in front of him.

I told Ron – look at the force. Describe it. Explain what it is.

So, for the first time, Ron actually tried to see the force. He was expecting something large and scary and awful.

Except, when Ron really tried to look for it, all he could see was a shadow. As the shadow moved closer to him and more into the light, it gradually faded away, until there was nothing left at all.

When Ron did this, I watched tension leave his face. He became more relaxed, calmer. Happier.

Still with his eyes closed, in his mind's eye he walked out of the garage and went into his home. After our talk, Ron hasn't had the dream since.

Why did I tell that story? Because it illustrates the futility of resistance. And yet, despite it being the least effective way to process something, it's the most popular method we use to process everything.

Or at least it was for me.

This is a common workday for me.

I'll perceive a slight from a colleague – it could be something minor, but I'd inexcusably and inexplicably take it personally.

Then, after carrying it around for an hour or so, I'd tell myself to get rid of it. To think of something else; it was a waste of time.

Except that never worked. It just kept coming back and back. Resistance was futile.

Same goes for my fears. For example, despite flying often, I don't like flying. I'm scared of crashing and dying.

Whenever I fly, I tell myself not to think that way. I'd tell myself all the reasons I shouldn't think that way.

But it keeps coming back. Resistance was futile.

In martial arts, one of the things they teach you is to use your enemy's force against them. For instance, if they try to punch you, you can use their forward force to throw them the direction they're punching in.

I began applying that lesson to these thoughts and saw much better results. Now, when something bothers me, whether it be physical or mental pain or fear, I go toward it, not against it. And do my best to understand it by asking myself why I feel that way.

Often, just doing that eliminates it or shrinks it significantly. The rapid eye movement discussed in the previous chapter is a good final touch to cut it off completely, once you've distilled it down to the true root cause.

As I started doing this more and more, I began seeing a trend in what I was resisting the most. The answer – literally, nothing. Or, perhaps nothingness, to be more accurate.

Let's say death, something we all resist. The last thing anyone wants to think about is their own death. To make us feel better about it, we tell ourselves stories of it, and then endlessly distract ourselves with other pursuits so we don't think of the inevitable.

But why, exactly, are we scared of death?

I suppose the pain of dying is somewhat part of it. That seems legitimate. But even a peaceful death is scary. Why?

Because it's over. Because it's done. Worst case – the world moves on, we are forgotten and we become nothing.

Why is this scary? How can you be scared of nothing?

Except that's exactly what we are scared of most. Nothing.

A more pedestrian example is imposter syndrome, which is this feeling at work many people get (myself included) that you're an imposter. The fear is, unless we constantly put on airs and prove ourselves, we'll be found out as the imposters we are and be exposed as being nothing.

Once again, literally scared of nothing. We want to be something! Because if we are nothing, it means this whole thing is meaningless.

Why? Why is being meaningless scary?

I suppose, the reason meaningless or nothingness is scary is we'd like to think this world is for something. That our actions have consequences. That we matter.

But say, for the sake of argument, your life is meaningless – arguably the worst-case scenario. Why is this such a horrible thought?

Here's all it would mean – your life is yours and yours alone. You can do with it what you choose. You will die and you will be forgotten. So, with the limited time you have, you might as well live the absolute best life possible.

That sounds good, not bad. It comes with a lightness of being.

That means even the worst-case scenario isn't so bad. In fact, all the pain we're feeling isn't from the outcome at all – it's from the uncertainty of the outcome. Or, our refusal to accept the outcome.

Here's the point – our instinct is to fight, particularly fight things we don't understand or refuse to accept. But all of that fighting just causes us more pain and gets us nowhere.

Instead, just by seeing whatever we're resisting for what it is causes our suffering to fade. Because often, when you really boil it down, our resistance is – quite literally – over nothing.

THE SHORTCOMING
OF MEDITATION

In the 1860s, the biggest infrastructure project in the United States was the construction of the transcontinental railroad. With it, the United States would be fully connected, and no longer would people heading to California have to take a wagon across parts of the country.

This obviously was a massive project in a time before widespread machinery, meaning a lot of people had to do backbreaking manual labor to get it done. Most of these people were Chinese immigrants who flocked to California in hopes of finding gold, settling on low-paying jobs lying railroad track instead.

The owners of these railroads were demanding, the hours were long, the work was both boring and impossibly hard, and it was incredibly dangerous. For all of those reasons, in the beginning, many of these Chinese immigrants didn't do the job for very long.

To help, the railroad supervisors began supplying these Chinese laborers with their drug of choice, opium. This made it all far more bearable, retention went up and the work eventually got done. This was despite the inhumane conditions and the rampant racism of the railroad owners, who paid the Chinese workers far less than their white counterparts.

Hard non sequitur to modern times. While around for centuries, meditation is clearly having its moment in America. And, for good reason – there are studies that show meditation leads to less stress, better relationships, more happiness, better health; it's overwhelming.

I, per mandate of being a tech worker for a California-based company, also have been meditating on and off for several years. And I agree with the research – I've found, in my own life, I'm happier, I'm more calm, I get sick less and I am more compassionate to others if I regularly meditate.

It really does make your life better; I fully support.

That said, I believe there are clear shortcomings of meditation that are rarely discussed. And meditation, on its own, isn't a path anywhere. It's just merely a relatively effective tool.

Here's what I mean.

First off, let's talk about what meditation is, or at least what I understand meditation to be.

Meditation, as I was taught, is the process of focusing on your breath for an extended period of time. The goal is to let thoughts come and go and not become attached to them, like watching cars go by on the freeway.

If your mind slips up and you start thinking about something, it's okay. You just let go of the thought and refocus your mind on your breath, a process which meditation experts claim is the mental equivalent of a bicep curl.

Usually, people will do this for five to 10 minutes. There's also guided meditation, where someone basically tells you what to focus on. And then there's transcendental meditation, where you chant the same thing over and over, so you focus on that chant, not your breath.

The benefit of all of these forms of mediation is to disconnect you from your thoughts. This makes you less emotional and more compassionate, generally. It can also give you a sense of calm and make your life simpler.

All of these things are good. I've personally seen these benefits myself after meditating. I wouldn't say meditating regularly changed my life, but it did help me become more calm, less emotional and be more aware of the people around me.

What I just described sounds pretty good, right? Well, it is, and it's not particularly difficult to fit into your day. I'd recommend it to anyone; in the same way I'd recommend a healthy diet and exercise.

And that's really what meditation is – exercise for your mind. It makes your mind stronger, which lets you focus better and stops making you a victim to your emotions.

But that's all it is.

The problem, I see, is when meditation is treated as the be-all, end-all. It isn't, in the same way exercising regularly isn't the be-all, end-all.

Specifically, people who meditate often likely have all the benefits I already mentioned. They have a healthier mind.

The question is – what will you do with that healthier mind?

In tech, which attracts a lot of people whose false-self is tied strongly to their career, the message is simple: Meditate and you'll have a stronger mind. With that stronger mind, you'll be more productive and advance your career faster.

My question – so what?

You've advanced your career and now have a bigger job. What exactly does that get you? More stress? More hollow confidence in yourself? More money, but will that larger paycheck actually make you happier?

I've also heard about meditation being used essentially as a coping mechanism. Life is tough; meditate and it'll get better. You can use it to refocus your mind on positive things and the bad things won't seem so bad.

That, to me, is bogus. If your life sucks, go into the pain and understand it – most likely, it's because you are holding onto false beliefs. It might take some time, but once you do that, you'll eventually be able to let it go.

At this point, you might be wondering – why did he tell that story about Chinese immigrants at the beginning taking opium?

Here's why – those guys who built those railroads had rough lives, slaving away for hours for barely any money. The opium made it a bit easier, I suppose, but it didn't actually improve anything for them. The next day they still had to get back to work.

In the same way, our minds can be as demanding and exhausting as those railroad jobs. We are constantly telling ourselves we aren't good enough. We are constantly seeking external things to make us feel better internally, whether it be a date or a nice word from someone else or ice cream. We are constantly complaining about the outside world, blaming it for internal fears we have.

Our minds constantly put us in pain. And rather than breaking free of our minds, we look externally for things to fix what our mind has caused.

Sure, you could take opium to numb the pain your mind is causing you. Or, you could meditate, which might have a similar effect, without the negative side effects.

But you still are in pain. You still are, as Socrates would say, living an unexamined life, where fears masked as expectations and desires are driving your life.

Only by committing to serious reflection and full honesty with yourself can you rid yourself of all of that and get rid of this false self. The only way to get out of pain is to address the cause of it. In the same way you cannot fix a leaky pipe by taking a drive to Dairy Queen, you can't be happy without getting rid of what's making you unhappy.

Meditation can help you on this journey because it can help focus your mind. No different than how coffee can help you get there by giving you energy in the morning. Or a pen and paper, so you can write down your thoughts.

But meditation isn't anything more than that. On its own, while it will make life a little easier, you won't get you anywhere with it. It's nothing more than a good tool to use while embarking on your own inner pursuit.

Bottom line, should you meditate every day? Probably. But don't confuse that with growth.

WHAT "SEINFELD" SAYS ABOUT THE MEANING OF LIFE

Recently, Netflix agreed to buy the rights for "Seinfeld" for $500 million – $500 million! – for a five-year deal, starting in 2021. For a show that hasn't aired in 23 years and, I'm assuming, many people have already seen.

But I don't need that stat to tell you "Seinfeld" is perhaps the most popular and influential television show ever. The characters, from the stalwarts like Elaine to George to Kramer, to even the bit players like the Soup Nazi and David Puddy, will live on for decades. It was the first of its kind, it was razor-sharp, it pushed the envelope; it was brilliance.

It's also my personal favorite show of all time and it still makes me laugh hard, even though I've seen every episode at least four times.

Okay, not exactly new information here – "Seinfeld" is popular. We get it.

What's more interesting is exploring why it's popular.

When you ask people why they love "Seinfeld," they tend to say the same thing – it's relatable. The same things we all worry about and the same stupid situations we all get in are highlighted in the show.

There's even an expression that everything in life can relate to a "Seinfeld" episode. That's a bit of an exaggeration ... but not by much.

Concurrently, let's take a look at the premise of the show. The premise is famous – it's the show about nothing. Nothing!

Not literally nothing, I suppose, things happen in the show. But figuratively nothing.

The situations the actors get into almost never have lasting stakes or, even if they do, they don't seem to mind much anyway. Even when they talk about serious topics – Nazis, the electric chair, death, on and on – they bring up the most inane, inconsequential topics about those situations (example – George wondering what Civil War soldiers used for toilet paper).

And the characters never learn anything or improve, they never transcend the self-created situations they get themselves into. The best example of this – the first conversation of the show and the last conversation in the show are exactly the same, with Jerry criticizing the location of the second button on George's shirt.

We watched these characters for nine years get into all sorts of adventures, from Kramer being charged with murder to Jerry and George doing a pilot for NBC to George's fiancée dying to Elaine's up-and-down career to the incalculable amounts of breakups and disappointments, ending with the four of them being thrown in jail. And yet, despite all of that, they are still talking about the same stupid things.

They haven't grown at all.

Okay, let's rewind the past few paragraphs back. "Seinfeld" is one of the most popular shows ever because it's perhaps the most re-latable show ever. And yet, it's a show about completely meaning-less drivel, where the characters, despite a lifetime of ridiculous situations, learn nothing and wind up exactly where they started.

Let that sink in for a minute.

This is what we relate to as a society. We relate to nothing. We relate to meaninglessness. We relate to never transcending our own neuroses, never really going anywhere, and ending our run in the exact same spot we started it.

Pretty depressing, right?

Honestly, it should be depressing. Any piece of enduring art, whether it be a painting or a sculpture or a sitcom, endures because it tells the truth.

"Seinfeld" unapologetically told the truth – most of us live a life devoid of meaning. Most of us don't grow at all.

And it endures exactly for that reason.

I know – this isn't exactly an inspiring essay so far. Let's make it even more depressing by talking about combat veterans.

While not the case for all, many combat veterans have difficulty reacquainting to civilian life because of the banality of it. Being in battle is obviously awful, but it's also about as invigorating as an experience a person can have. There's no pontificating, there's no wondering about the greater meaning of life, there's no downtime or arguments about a shirt button; there's nothing other than trying to survive and accomplish a mission.

It's intense and it feels incredibly meaningful, literally a life-and-death situation. Contrast that to coming back home and having conversations about what color to paint the living room or what to serve at the dinner party.

This meaninglessness, the exact meaninglessness Seinfeld depicts so perfectly, crushes these veterans. They crave the intensity they felt in combat, often trying to re-create it by partying hard, via daredevil stunts, driving motorcycles, whatever. But nothing compares, and it leaves a perpetual void.

While combat veterans feel this more acutely because they've experienced the exact opposite of the mind-numbing frivolousness of daily life, I think we've all had this feeling. This frustrating boredom of daily living, this overwhelming desire to feel something.

It's that exact feeling that causes us to wonder what this is all about, anyway. It makes us ask – why exactly are we here? What's the point?

Yup, here's where I explain what the meaning of life is. Buckle up.

I think "Seinfeld" shows us exactly what the meaning of life isn't. And, while I'm sure Jerry Seinfeld and Larry David would hate to admit the show was even the slightest bit philosophical, I think it was profoundly so. Their message – life is meaningless and most of us don't really grow at all.

Not exactly an inspiring message. But, perhaps, what it really means is – the normal life many of us lead is indeed meaningless. It's an essay on what not to do. The challenge is going beyond that.

Most of us ignore this warning, spending an inordinate amount of time – perhaps 90% of our day, perhaps 100% – thinking, worrying or doing things that have absolutely no meaning. The exact type of things George, Jerry, Elaine and Kramer do, which ultimately lead nowhere.

I can list out countless examples here. Our work, specifically our unending desire to move up and make more money, is basically meaningless. Anything related to anything material is clearly meaningless. The many small desires we have, like trying to impress others or win a game of cards, are meaningless.

To counteract this, we try desperately to add meaning to things where there is none. Or, we simply dull that feeling, either through drugs or sports or gambling or the million other ways available to us, to distract ourselves from ourselves.

So, you are probably thinking right now – okay, hot shot. What's meaningful?

I think, to answer that question, you first need to scrape away all the meaninglessness inside your brain. And that in itself is a lot of work.

That requires you getting rid of your many desires to impress others, the constant desire to make more and more money, our many petty grievances, etc. It requires you to be brutally honest with yourself, to ask yourself why and why again until you get to the true root cause – which is always a fear. And then, facing that fear and letting it go.

What's left after you strip away all that is meaningless?

I personally can't say, because I'm still in the process of doing it. But if you listen to the very few people who have reached that state, they'll tell you it's the end of self. And instead, we reach what we really are, which is something far beyond skin, bones and brain.

Here's the point – you can spend your days climbing Mount Kilimanjaro or making millions of dollars or mastering calligraphy or watching television in your sweats, it doesn't really matter. All of that stuff is the "Seinfeld" approach, where you do a lot of distracting things but never go anywhere.

Or you can grab a pen and paper and ask yourself why you want to do any of those things. Begin to question who you are and the many fears that drive what you do and how you feel each day.

Begin to strip away all the fears that make you do the things you do.

Why is this meaningful, compared to anything else? Because here you are getting closer to the truth, instead of getting further intertwined in the many non-truths. Here, you take full control over your own life, and become the person you really are – instead of the false-self many of us let dominate our lives.

P.S. The "Seinfeld" finale.

I get it, it wasn't that funny. But, looking back, the concept is genius.

The whole episode is an allegory of the final judgment.

I believe the characters actually die in the plane crash. And then, they face St. Peter at the gates of heaven to see which direction they are headed – north or south.

In the episode, this judgment is done literally by a judge, as the impact of their lives is analyzed in court. The verdict is unanimous – the characters haven't grown at all, they've been selfish their whole lives and they are bad people.

Hence, they are sentenced to jail for a year, which is an obvious metaphor for hell.

Despite this, as they sit in jail, George, Jerry, Elaine and Kramer are still not inspired to change, having the exact same conversation they had before. The assumption is that even after they are released again into the world (perhaps a metaphor for reincarnation?), they will be no different than where they left off, doomed to live the same life again and again and again.

The point Larry David and Jerry Seinfeld are making: Don't let this be you. Don't spend your life in this crippling neurosis. It's a path quite literally to hell.

Pretty brilliant, right? I think so, even if the jokes don't land.

THE TOXICITY OF DISTRACTION

I have a challenge for you.

Go to a room by yourself, sit there for an hour and don't say or do anything. Don't check your phone, don't read a book. In fact, try not to think of anything.

Not meditation, where you focus on your breath. Just sit quietly and do nothing.

This sounds like the easiest challenge in the history of mankind. And yet, I'll bet you will find it extremely difficult.

Here's what will start to happen when you do this – your mind will go crazy. Your thoughts will speed up. You'll have urges to do something – watch television, check your phone, even to complete mindless tasks like taking out the trash or cleaning that leftover dish in the sink. These urges will get stronger and stronger, as you feel the need to do something.

To be productive. To accomplish a task!

Now, I have another challenge for you. Spend an hour watching television by yourself. Or surfing the web. Or playing a video game or reading a murder mystery.

This, I suspect, will be much, much easier for you. In fact, I'll bet you've spent at least an hour watching television or surfing the web in the last 24 hours. And while you might have had some tinges to get things done, the urges to be productive aren't nearly as strong as if you were to just sit quietly by yourself.

What's changed in these two scenarios?

In the latter, where you watch a screen for an hour, your energy is focused outward — on something somebody else is doing. Essentially, the screen serves as a distraction for you from yourself for an hour, and that makes you feel content.

In the former, where you sit alone, you remove that distraction. And you are forced to look inward into your actual thoughts.

And we, generally speaking, don't like doing that.

I'll use myself as an example. Until March 2020, I spent almost all of my time distracting myself from myself. I'd wake up and immediately have Alexa tell me the news as I got dressed. Then, as I took the subway to work, I'd listen to a sports podcast on my headphones. At work, I obviously worked. But even when there was downtime, I'd spend that time surfing the web or chatting with my colleagues.

When I got home, my mind was usually fried, and yet I'd usually keep a podcast on as I cooked and ate dinner. After, I'd generally put on the television, although I didn't really watch it and mostly just played around on my phone.

Even when I hung out with friends, we mostly talked about all the information I took in that day, i.e., sports, news or TV. And, when the conversation hit a lull, I'd pull out my phone to distract myself again.

Let me be clear – television or video games or podcasts or novels are all fine. But why did I feel the need to distract myself almost every minute of the day with them?

Because your mind doesn't want you to look inside, and it fights any effort to do so. And it's very effective at this; or, at least, mine is.

What will happen if you stop constantly distracting yourself? And why do we feel this need to do it in the first place?

I'll start with the what, because that'll sound pretty good. And then I'll cover the why, which might spook some people.

First, what you get when you stop constantly distracting yourself. If you make more time to sit in silence, you will be less stressed, happier, have a better perspective and be far more creative. Ever wonder why people say they think of their best ideas in the shower?

That's because the shower is the only time of the day many of us have where we aren't distracting ourselves and actually have room to think. If you make more time like that, you will generate better, more prosperous ideas.

If you keep giving yourself that time, you'll get a better sense of what you aren't, which will bring you closer to who you really are. And that will lead to truly lasting happiness.

In summary, if you spend more time with yourself with no distraction, you'll be mentally healthier, probably richer, have a better understanding of the world and happier. Sounds pretty good, right?

Well, it is.

That's the benefit. What's more interesting is the why. And, equally important, why your mind will literally fight you when you try to spend time quietly with yourself.

As in, when you try to sit quietly for any extended period of time, your mind will go haywire thinking of things to do and urging you to be distracted by something. Anything. Why does it do this?

Well, generally things fight to avoid losing power. And that's exactly what your mind is afraid of – losing power over you.

As discussed in the past chapter, your mind isn't who you are – you are something behind that. Your mind is merely a tool you have, no different than an arm or a leg, that's evolved over time.

But your mind is a very powerful tool that convinces you it is indeed more than a tool; it is something real. Psychologists call this the "ego." Sitting quietly reduces the ego's power and gives you time to connect to the real you, which your ego hates.

So what does the ego do? It fights in an effort to stay in control. Don't listen; it's just the ego, which is really nothing more than a clump of attachments.

Sitting quietly is one method to getting rid of the ego; even better is to write down your thoughts. This focuses the mind and forces you to get to the root causes of your mental suffering.

If you journal when your mind is going particularly crazy, you'll feel better. If you journal consistently, you'll make real progress.

Here's the bigger point – all of the things your ego urges you to do are external. It's focused on making more money or watching television or proving yourself or cleaning the house or even helping someone else. But you cannot progress if you are always looking externally.

The ego doesn't want you to progress because it wants to keep the chains of power it has over you. It fights this via distraction, which manifests itself in watching television, mindless conversations, petty grievances and a thousand other ways.

That's not to say that watching television or small talk is bad – it isn't. It's when you are doing these things compulsively that it becomes an issue, and that's exactly what happens to most of us – we are compulsively living distracted lives to avoid the struggle of looking inward.

That leads to a lot of people doing a lot of stuff and not getting anywhere. Sure, they may have climbed the highest mountain and made millions of dollars, but they haven't progressed one inch.

I'm far more impressed with someone who has diminished or – very rarely – eliminated their ego. That's a true victory and leads to legitimate and lasting self-actualization, compared to the ephemeral relief any external pursuit provides.

I'll end with this. Want a truly epic challenge?

No need to fight in a war or circumvent the globe in a hot air balloon or memorize all the words to "We Didn't Start the Fire." Those are mere distractions.

Instead, sit down, shut up, grab a pen and confront the monster within.

HOW TO DEAL WITH THE HEAVIEST EMOTION

Every emotion is felt by the body in a different way.

Pain is sharp and biting, with a desire to lash out. Anxiety is also sharp and biting, but with a desire to lash within. Sadness is like your body turning into stone, making every step seem impossible.

These are all bad. All must be shed, as all release toxins that will destroy your body over time.

Although often, emotions like anger and anxiety and even sadness are symptoms of a more destructive emotion that destroys the human spirit. Robs us of our joy. And is unquestionably the heaviest of all emotional sensations we feel.

That emotion is guilt. An emotion I carried around for so many years and was the root cause of so many other destructive emotions.

Before I went on this journey within, I was always vacillating between feeling anger and feeling anxious. After I started clearing my mind, I spent several months removing both anger and anxiety, only to determine both were just manifestations of the guilt I was carrying around inside.

Once I realized that, my focus changed to defeating guilt. My first step there – understanding what guilt is.

Sure, I knew what guilt felt like. After all, I had carried around different forms of guilt all of my life. But I didn't really understand what guilt was.

So, I began to dig. I knew what caused guilt: doing something wrong. But why did doing something wrong make me feel guilty?

To figure that out, I started analyzing the feelings around the guilt – which is really a persistent feeling of "I should've …" or "I shouldn't …".

For example, I should've been nicer to the customer service rep. I shouldn't have made fun of that person behind their back. I should've remembered that person's birthday.

Additionally, I realized guilt stayed with me far longer than other emotions. Anger, for instance, came and went. But guilt persisted.

That's when it clicked and I understood what guilt really is: denial. Persistent denial. And that meant the antidote to guilt was obvious: acceptance.

I realized that to solve guilt, I had to accept what happened. It's that simple.

I'll give an example to illustrate my point.

A couple of years ago, an older man I'm friends with got into a motorcycle accident and suffered a severe neck injury. After a week in the hospital and then several weeks recovering at home, he was able to walk again, and he had me and several other people over to his home for dinner to celebrate.

Our friend was wearing a neck brace and was taking painkillers, which made him a bit woozy. After dinner, we were sitting around his coffee table and he stood up and walked over to get a bowl of chips. My feet were in his path, I was talking with someone else, and he tripped over them.

Thankfully, a person was alert and caught him before he fell. Otherwise, he would've seriously injured himself. Maybe even died.

Thank god he was okay. But I felt incredible guilt about tripping him, which I carried for several years. In my mind, all I wanted was to redo that moment and move my feet out of his path. I kept replaying in my head what I should've done.

To move past this, I had to accept what happened – I wasn't paying attention. I tripped him. And nearly killed him.

That's what happened; nothing I can do about it.

It's therapeutic, in this moment, to write that out. It's full acceptance of what actually happened. And it also makes the lesson of the situation obvious – I need to be more aware of my surroundings.

Now, the truth is, I've done far worse things than accidentally trip a man. But still, the process is the same.

That's one form of guilt, which is usually brought on by a horrible outcome. There's also another form of guilt I needed to shed, which was far more common and persistent.

This guilt revolved around my relationships with other people.

What do I mean by this?

Here's one example. Previously, when I hung out with people socially, I almost always had a headache afterward.

This headache, I later realized, was caused by guilt.

See, when I hang out with people socially, I really want them to have a good time. I put pressure on myself to be "on" and to keep them entertained the whole night.

After the night would end, I'd beat myself up for all the perceived mistakes I made. Wish I would've said this or said that, done this or done that. I'd literally feel guilty about not being entertaining enough.

To remove this guilt, I needed to come clean with myself and accept the truth. Yes, I wasn't entertaining every minute of the night. Maybe the people did have a bad time. So what?

Perhaps they'd never hang out with me again, sure. But, honestly, the bigger issue is why am I putting so much pressure on myself in the first place. I'm not responsible for them having a good time; I'm only responsible for myself having a good time. And this pressure is robbing me of that.

That realization helped me shed my guilt in social situations.

Beyond feelings of guilt from hanging out with people generally, there were specific people in my life who made me feel guilty. People who I believed were struggling and I needed to "save."

First step: Accept the reality of them and their situation, which removes the guilt.

Meaning, often, I saw people I cared about who were struggling with some demon. Rather than accept them and the situation they were in, I was constantly wishing they would magically rid themselves of all impurities and never be sad again.

This is a form of guilt, because I wasn't accepting who they actually are and the situation they're in. I was always wishing for it to change. This puts the person on the defensive and makes you unable to help in a meaningful way.

The second thing I began to realize is, yes, they're struggling. But then again – aren't I struggling too?

It was ironic, really. Here I was, feeling guilty about other people's struggles. And yet, I had my own struggles in front of me that I wasn't addressing.

It reminds me of these conversations I have with this couple I'm close with. I'll talk to the husband one-on-one, and he'll list the things he wishes his wife would work on, and how he feels bad for her. Then I'll talk to the wife one-on-one, and she'll list the things her husband should work on, and how she feels bad for him.

They both feel guilty about something they have no control over while ignoring their own issues, which they have complete control over. I always laugh to myself when they start doing this.

And yet, I was doing the exact same thing.

The realization: I needed to stop trying to save other people. They will do what they do, and all I can do is accept them for who they are.

Instead, I realized I needed to focus on what I actually have control over, which is "saving" myself.

As I continued on this journey, I began to see how much guilt I was carrying around in my mind. Which is to say, how much mind space I was dedicating to rethinking what I should've said or done in various situations from my past.

This, I'm now realizing, is complete madness. I cannot change the past. I must accept it.

I admit, accepting my full past can be painful at times. There are some dark things I'd rather not address. But it's far better than wasting my life trying to redo something that already happened.

The good news? By accepting the difficult parts of my past, I'm able to quickly glean insights from those mistakes. And that's further helped me remove attachments and clear my mind.

The point: Guilt is just denial. The reason it's so heavy is because the denial prevents us from processing the reality of the situation in a meaningful way.

To process reality, we must first accept reality, which sheds the guilt. And then, as we process what happened, we can learn from it and move forward.

DEATH, MY BEST FRIEND

I will die.

One day, I will die, and I probably will be buried in the ground. My body will rot, the memory of me will fade, and within 100 years or so – likely much less – I shall forever be forgotten.

That will be that. There's no avoiding it, there's no denying it, there's no nothing. Death is truth.

When will it happen? Could happen this afternoon. Could happen next week. Perhaps I'll go to the doctor next Friday for what I think is slight back pain, only to discover it's an untreatable tumor and I have but a few weeks to live.

Or maybe I'll live another 60 years and die a weathered old man with no memories of my life. Doesn't really matter when, the important thing is I will die, and it could happen any moment.

There's no greater gift than this. Nothing in this world makes sense than knowing I will die.

Why?

It focuses my mind. By always fully accepting the reality of death, and thinking through the moments right before I die, I get such clarity about what's true and what's not.

There are beliefs I'm holding onto right now which, in the moments before my death, I will know are lies. For years, I've defended these beliefs, advocated for these beliefs.

And yet, thinking through my death, I know they are not true. I shall let go of these thoughts.

Thinking about death reveals to me who I really am, as what remains after is the real me. Perhaps that's nothing – if so, this whole thing is just a puppet show, which is a freeing thought.

I shall enjoy it. It's a good show. No need to get too attached to it, though, as all the puppets on stage get put in the same box when it's all done.

By putting myself in the last moments of my death, I know where to put my energy. There are so many things that I currently think about, talk about and do that are destructive and take me further away from the truth.

I shall stop doing these things.

By thinking about my death, I know what the true purpose of life is. Is it, as Orwell wrote, to build things just to destroy them, to fight an endless war in the search for peace? Obviously not, but that's what I used to do, because I lived an unexamined life.

Now, as I reflect on death, I know what life is really about. Why it's such a gift, and how to make the most out of it. And what to get rid of.

I'd rather not die today, because I'm enjoying this too much. But if death comes today, I shall embrace it, as I know it's my time. I know I've done whatever it is I'm supposed to do.

For years, I thought death was the enemy, too terrible to think about. I've kept making distractions and telling myself stories so I wouldn't look at death perched on my shoulder.

Now, death is my friend. My greatest friend, in fact. A powerful shredder that rips through all that doesn't serve me.

One day, perhaps as soon as today, I will really get to meet death. I'm a bit curious to know what he brings.

In the interim, I keep him with me every day. I think about him whenever my mind gets busy or life appears tough. Never does he not come through and show me the way.

What better friend could I ask for?

THE PARADOX OF OUTCOMES, AND WHY LIFE ISN'T BASEBALL

Until a few days ago, the more I wrote this book, the more anxious I became.

This isn't my first book. Not even close. My first book was also a book of essays, called *Thoughts from an Insecure Egomaniac*, which I wrote when I was 22. It actually isn't bad – I'm proud of most of them. But I never tried to publish it, never even really finished it.

My first true book I self-published in 2016. It was a novel called *Dan Berith and the Plight of the Lions*. And it was bad. Not just because it was poorly written and had virtually no plot.

But it was an angry book, with nothing really to say, filled with needless expletives. The worst part – after I published it, I told all my friends and family to buy it, and many did.

Including my grandma, which is pretty embarrassing considering the book features a stripper and half a dozen "romance" scenes. To be honest, I wish that book never happened, but it is what it is.

My second book was nicer and a bit better, without any swear words. Still though, not very good: a CIA thriller, without the thrill.

I tried to get this book to a publisher, which starts with getting a literary agent. I sent it to more than 25 and only heard back from one.

What did the one say? A one-word response: "Nope." I followed up and asked why. The guy said simply wrote, "Not impressed by the writing. At all."

Sooo, not good.

In the two years that followed, I've started and stopped writing at least seven other novels. Some I got more than 100 pages into, others just a few chapters. Each one I gave up, knowing there was nothing there. I was afraid of failing again.

At the start of 2020, I promised myself I wouldn't try to write any more novels. It was time to move on; it wasn't in the cards for me. I'd never be a writer.

Ten months later, I started writing this book. In fairness, it's a book of essays, not another novel. But still, a book nonetheless.

I have more confidence in this one. Mostly, because I'm writing it not to become a famous writer, which was my motivation for the other books. Instead, it's because I legitimately wanted to share what I had learned, as it has been so life-changing for me.

That said, the hauntings of all those failures remained with me. I didn't want to fail again; I didn't want all of this work to go for naught. The thoughts became paralyzing.

About a week ago, I heard the right message from the right teacher. He told me that this fear derived from outcome-based thinking, and that outcome-based thinking was robbing me of both potential and my joy.

Once I realized that he was right, I adopted a new approach with a clear mind. Let me explain.

There tend to be two types of people in this world: people who dwell on the past and people who dwell on the future. Neither is healthy.

I was very much the type of person who dwells on the future. Specifically, I was constantly doing things for the outcome I was excited to get from them.

For example, working out. I wasn't working out because I liked working out. I was working out because I was excited how my body would eventually look.

Work was a better example. I constantly was working really hard with the dreams of where that one day would lead. I figured, sure it sucks now, but it's going to be sweet once I'm filthy rich and living in my mansion.

That's outcome-based thinking in a nutshell. I was ignoring the present for the hopes of better days ahead.

The downsides of this approach?

First off, those better days never seemed to come. I was always chasing some new outcome, some new pursuit. I was the type of person who would climb Mount Everest and think, sure, that was cool, but maybe next time I'll bring a ladder and get a little bit higher still.

Second, as reflected in my experience in writing this book, I had an intense fear of failure. I was petrified of not getting that outcome. That fear of failure ultimately leads to stifled creativity and, ironically, worse outcomes.

Third, and most importantly, it's not the best way to live. I was never really in the present moment. Instead, I was always focused on where the actions in that moment would take me. I wasn't enjoying and making the most out of the here and now, which is really what life is about.

I'll add a fourth negative as well. Because I was so focused on out-comes, I often defined myself by my outcomes. That means if my outcomes were good, I'd feel good. But if the outcomes were bad, I'd feel bad.

That's giving away my power.

In summary – discontent, insecure and bad outcomes. Not a good way to live life.

To solve this problem, I needed to understand why my thinking was so focused on outcomes. And, as I did that, I realized this men-tal approach was a lot like playing baseball.

In baseball, the idea is to go from base to base. Sure, while you are running toward a base, people can tag you out. But, once you get on a base, you're safe.

Outcome-based thinking is the same. The idea is, sure, you've got to run through hell. But, once you hit a specific goal, you'll be good. You'll be safe.

The only problem – there are no "bases" in life. There's no safe place. I was running after something that doesn't exist, so the feel-ing of insecurity was with me no matter where I went. That causes anxiety.

Plus, as I was running toward this figurative base, I wasn't think-ing about the best way to get there. I was far too scared to do any of that. Instead, I just relied on what I was comfortable doing already, only learning something new if I absolutely had to.

This caused me to live a very rote, predictable life, filled with rote, predictable outcomes. I was so afraid of failure, I wasn't willing to try new things or challenge myself. I got to a point where I would get good enough to get a decent outcome and just kept doing it over and over, too afraid to change course.

Sure, this could lead to some success, but there's a cap to it. I never was going to reach my full potential with this approach. I needed to be willing to accept failure or else I never would really grow.

Ultimately, I was really running away from a fear, a fear I stupidly thought I could solve by accomplishing something external. That's obviously not true; the only way to get rid of any fear is to fight the battle within.

Once I realized where this outcome-based thinking was coming from, I needed to start countering it. And that meant facing the fears I was running away from.

I started with accepting the failure of this book. That meant facing the worst possible outcome: The book wouldn't be successful. That would put me in, well, the exact position I already am.

Not that scary. I have nothing to lose, baby!

That helped me drop the anxiety for the book, at the very least. But then I started exploring other areas where I had more to lose.

A big one for me – my job. I have a steady, secure job. How could I possibly face losing it?

Here's a better question. My job is how I spend the majority of my life. Why should I be scared of doing it?

One more example, to bring the point home. I'm a decent tennis player. To become a better tennis player, I'd need to hit my forehand and backhand harder.

Now, with my current ability, I can get my forehand and backhand very consistently, but neither shot has the power to take me to the next level.

I'm afraid of hitting the ball harder because I'll be less accurate and be worse in the short term. And I'm afraid of that outcome, because it means I'll lose some matches, which will make me feel embarrassed and less-than.

To move forward, I need to shed this fear of losing and getting embarrassed, as even that worst-case scenario isn't really that bad. Only by accepting that I might be bad, do I give myself the opportunity to start getting good.

So, what's the opposite of an outcome-based mindset? Having no goals and just drifting through life?

Not at all. First off, I started actively removing my fear of failure. Meaning, before I do anything, I accept that I might fail at it and get through the worst-case scenario.

That gives me the freedom to be creative and try new things, as I've already processed the worst outcome. Over time, as I eradicate the fear of failure again and again, it'll eventually disappear.

Second, I began focusing on just doing my best. If my best doesn't lead to success, that's fine – much more important is knowing, in my heart, that I legitimately did everything I could.

That puts the focus on the process instead of the outcome.

Third, I still make goals, but they are more holistic and less specific. For example, instead of saying "I want to get this exact job title at this exact salary," I'll say, "I want to enjoy my job and make a good living doing it."

With the first goal, I might get that specific job title, but I'd be running after it. I'd be filled with anxiety as I do it, I'd miss other opportunities as I chase after it and, if I actually did get it, I wouldn't even find it particularly satisfying.

In the latter, which I've begun to adopt, I've taken more chances. My life feels fuller. And I've enjoyed the journey much more

That brings me to the ultimate irony I realized throughout this whole process: Once you start letting go of these outcomes, they tend to come to you.

You let go of this fear-based desire to meet someone, you suddenly are in a much better place to meet the right person. You let go of this fear-based desire to make money, and suddenly you start seeing opportunities to be prosperous more clearly. You let go of this fear-based desire to impress people, and suddenly people like hanging around you more.

That said, if you let go of things with hopes of getting them, you are missing the point. It's all about clearing your mind and living in your natural state – the most important thing is enjoying the now.

CONFRONTING MY DEMON WITH A THOUSAND FACES

I think almost everyone has a demon with 1,000 faces.

Meaning that fight we simply cannot shake. It might manifest itself in many ways – a boss, a spouse, your child or someone on social media – but it's that same damn struggle again and again. And again.

And again.

It follows us, stalks us and always causes us pain. It's our No. 1 foe, our biggest enemy.

Yet, it often lives in secret. And rarely is it challenged.

To that point – I'll bet you can identify that demon for most people in your life. Maybe you have a friend who doesn't have enough self-confidence, and that manifests itself in their relationships, their job, everything. Or, you have a sibling who always has to be right, and they have challenges related to that with person after person. You say to yourself, "Why can't that person just fix that?"

But real talk for a second: Do you know what your demon with 1,000 faces is? And even if you do, do you have a solution for it?

Well, I can tell you, I didn't really know what mine was until I was

36 (even though it had a profound effect on my life). And I certainly didn't have a solution for it.

That changed when I was going through the process of clearing my mind and a work conflict made my demon rise once again. This time, Jen and her mom called it out, and refused to let it slip into the shadows again. This time, with their guidance, I identified my persistent demon for what it was and finally confronted it.

Okay, so what's my demon with 1,000 faces? The one core struggle that keeps appearing in my life?

Well, I have a common one: people-pleasing. Making other people happy, afraid of rocking the boat. I kinda sorta knew this about myself for a while, but only after I seriously started clearing my mind did I understand how destructive it was.

And finally, I started figuring out how to overcome it.

Here's the drama that inspired this whole chapter – a conflict at work. A conflict caused by a colleague acting like a bully and trying to push me around.

The good news is that externally, I did everything right. I stayed professional, pushed back, told my manager, the whole deal. I checked all the boxes.

I learned how to react effectively over the years. That's the benefit of experience. You get better at handling things externally.

But internally, I was a mess.

Internally, despite this person being the clear cause of the problem, for some reason, to me, it was my fault. It was my fault they were telling me one thing and someone else another – I should've pushed harder for clarity. It was my fault they were acting like a bully – I should've been more assertive. It was my fault they lost their cool – I should've been more graceful.

Of course, none of those things was my fault. That person chose to act how they wanted to act and put me in that position to begin with. They lied, they got caught in the lie and then, rather than apologizing, they doubled down and tried to bully their way through.

It was clear to everyone involved that my colleague was out of line. But in my mind, somehow it was my fault that this person wasn't happy. It was my fault for not pleasing this person enough.

That weighed on me. I didn't sleep.

Again, this wasn't the first time I felt this way. I've experienced this same cycle countless times over my life, with countless people playing the role of my demon with 1,000 faces.

Except this time, Jen and her mom wouldn't let it die, as they saw the toll it was taking on me. They helped me finally understand what it was.

So what did I do in response once I realized what my demon was?

To begin with, I had to understand why this people-pleasing demon was so destructive. I centered on three big reasons.

First, despite my best efforts, obviously there was still conflict in my life. In fact, the act of avoiding conflict was just making the conflict in my life bigger and more dramatic.

Meaning, this whole approach wasn't working.

Second, I cannot control other people and outside circumstances, no matter what I do. There will always be external conflict, no matter how hard I try to avoid it.

Meaning, this whole approach was doomed to fail.

Third, by focusing on seeking an outcome from others, I wasn't living my own life. Instead, I was putting my energy into appeasing everyone else.

Meaning, I wasn't living my own dream, and there's no bigger crime than that. I need to chart my own path, not walk the path I believe others want me to take.

In summary, my people-pleasing compulsion was ineffective, impossible and idiotic. And yet, I kept doing it, and kept letting this demon with 1,000 faces dominate my life.

Why? The same reason we do every dumb thing – fear.

Okay, now we're getting to the root cause, which is where Jen really leaned in. She asked me – what did I fear, why was I so compelled to please others?

Well, quite obviously, I feared people not liking me. But why was I afraid of people not liking me?

It's actually very similar to the last chapter and the baseball metaphor – I figured if everyone likes me, I'll be safe. And then I won't have to worry about anything.

Except this isn't possible. There is no "safe space" and there will always be people who don't like me, no matter what I do or say.

So, really, it comes down to control. Am I willing to let go of my illusion of control and accept the world as it is, instead of what I'd like it to be?

Sounds like a no-brainer, right? But it's the hardest thing, taking your hand off the tiller. It's like letting go of the armrest during turbulence on a flight – you know gripping it isn't helping in any way, but it feels better than not doing it.

That's what I was doing with this whole people-pleasing thing – I was gripping onto something. When I broke it down, I realized it wasn't even the external conflict itself that was causing me pain, but my reaction to it. That act of gripping.

And really, to get all meta, that's what this whole book is about. It's about understanding and overcoming the ego, which is nothing more than our sad attempt to control what we cannot control.

Our ego is created when we refuse to surrender. It's nothing more than a bundle of fears that gets us nowhere.

I realized, going through this process, that I needed to surrender. To stop fighting. To stop opposing the world and myself and start accepting everything as it is.

To let go of my ego.

Previously, I thought by fighting, I was being tough. But I wasn't being tough at all. I was just being a scared little child.

The only way I could defeat my demon was to stop resisting it. To rest. And to allow this fear to blow right over me, like a plane flying right through a cloud.

Am I perfect? Do I do this all the time? Of course not. There are times the metaphorical plane starts shaking and I grab that metaphorical armrest again.

And that demon with 1,000 faces comes back into my life.

But I recognize it more now. And I tell myself that this attempt to control what I cannot control won't work and will only cause me pain.

Then, I do my best to let go. It's scary at times, but at least it's the truth. I take solace in that.

Plus, if I do it well, I feel something. Something I haven't felt since I was a child.

Peace. True inner peace.

And that feels good.

A GOOD EXERCISE
TO END ON

I've written about a lot of heavy topics in this book. Death, being alone, our biggest demons, the meaning (or meaninglessness) of life, the fundamental truth of the universe.

I wrote it because all of those things are critical to understanding who we are, why we're here and what we should do. I believe that framework gives us the ability to unlearn all the wrong beliefs, bad habits and unfounded attachments we gain throughout life, and become the free people we ought to be.

But before I go and let you be on your way, I want to end with an exercise that I think you'll enjoy. And it makes the point this whole book is trying to make, in a pleasant way.

It's quite easy too, all you need is some quiet.

All you have to do is go get comfortable. Sit in your favorite chair or lay down in your bed, doesn't matter. Close your eyes. Take a few deep breaths, focusing only on your inhale and exhale.

Then, imagine yourself when you are young. Say, 6 years old. All by yourself, in the woods alongside the water, playing and enjoying the day.

Feel how happy you are. Feel how free you are. No fears that you are alone, no pressure to impress anyone or to be productive, no worries about money or relationships or geopolitical issues.

Just witness the very young you, enjoying the fresh air and the pretty view of the water, enjoying the day.

Now imagine all the heaviness you've added since those days. Picture it all as one giant black ball you've built up over time and somehow made its way into your body.

Look at that black ball through the eyes of your 6-year-old self. And just watch it disappear, fading away like a cool ocean mist.

Go back to being the 6-year-old you, happy and free. Nothing to fear, nothing to do, nothing to hide.

Enjoy.

ACKNOWLEDGEMENTS

Don't think this book was created by just me. Many, many people were essential in crafting this work – I'd love to publicly acknowledge a few of them here.

Jen, obviously, who played a starring role in this book. Jen and I are no longer together, but she played a huge role in my life and we will always be friends.

Thank you.

Jen's mom also was essential to this journey. Thank you as well, Jen's mom. You are truly a bundle of joy.

Of course, I wouldn't even be in existence without my own parents, for whom I owe the world. Thank you both so much. If someone were to ask me if I hit the jackpot in the parents department, I'd be forced to raise both of my hands and proclaim, "Guilty as charged."

(Yes, that's an inside joke only my mother will get.)

Amy, John, Sam – I love you all very much, along with Shubert, Tyler, Erin, Zach, Brady, Willie, Catie, Olivia, Jack, Eva and Ellie. Thank you all for making me the person I am today.

A special shoutout to Susan Banning, who edited this book. Susan, you are the most talented editor I've ever worked with, and this book wouldn't have been possible without you. Thank you for another great effort.

All the people I've met over the years, and the many relationships I've had, all helped create this as well. In fact, some of the most difficult relationships I've endured have led to the biggest revelations. So, thank you all, even the people who drove me crazy.

Most of all, thank you, the reader. I sincerely hope you got something out of this book.

All the best and good luck on your own journey.

ABOUT THE AUTHOR

Paul Petrone

Paul Petrone currently lives and works in New York City.

Outside of work, Paul enjoys reading Jed McKenna, traveling to new places and being outside. Most of all, Paul wishes you luck on your own battle within.

Made in United States
North Haven, CT
28 September 2022

24665500R00049